P9-DFK-637

Meditations

Sylvia Browne

LIFE
Styles

Hay House, Inc.
Carlsbad, California • Sydney, Australia

Published and distributed in the United States by:
Hay House, Inc., P.O. Box 5100, Carlsbad, CA 92018-5100
(800) 654-5126 • (800) 650-5115 (fax)

Editorial: Jill Kramer • *Illustrations:* Caroline S.
Cover and Interior Design: Ashley Parsons

Library of Congress Cataloging-in-Publication Data

Browne, Sylvia.
    Meditations / Sylvia Browne.
        p. cm.
    ISBN 1-56170-719-8
1. Meditations. 2. Society of Novus Spiritus (Campbell, Calif.) I. Title.

BL624.2.B76 2000
299'.93—dc21   99-087364

ISBN 1-56170-719-8

04 03 02 01   5 4 3 2

1st printing, January 2001
2nd printing, January 2001

Printed in China Through Palace Press International

meditations

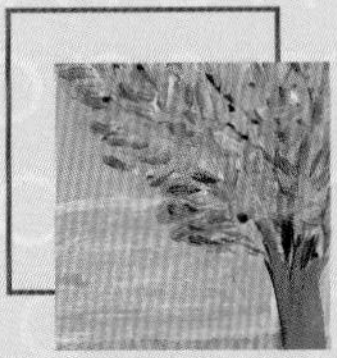

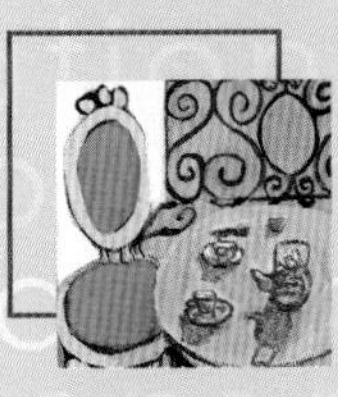

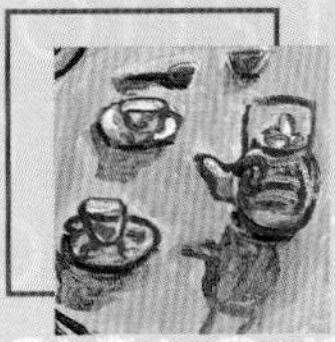

contents

meditations
meditations
meditations
meditations
meditations
meditations
meditations
meditations
meditations
meditations
meditations
meditations
meditations
meditations
meditations
meditations
meditations
meditations
meditations
meditations

How to Meditate

by Sylvia Browne

(Sylvia is the founder of the church called Society of
Novus Spiritus, located in Campbell, California.
The meditations in this book are based on the
tenets of her church.)

Quite a bit of the meditation process is
achieved through the senses. Many people
who are asked to visualize say that they don't
know how, or they've tried to do it without
much success. As I've said many times before,
if you can trace the route you've just driven
in your mind's eye, then you can visualize.
However, rarely do we visualize in living color.
This sometimes takes a great deal of practice.
After all, we are viewing from *within,* not with
our physical eyes.

We can also receive messages through
infusion, a process where a thought appears
in our minds. Many times we wonder where
it comes from. Simply put, when we quiet the
constant chatter of our minds, we open our
channels to unseen, loving companions along
the pathway of our lives. Our most constant
companion is our spirit guide, who is our

messenger from God. With practice, we can meet our guide through meditation.

Basically, prayer is asking something of God; meditation is listening for the answer. So, rid your mind of any preconceived notions about what to expect or experience. Use the following method of relaxation as a tool to prepare yourself for the meditations in this book, then let the beauty flow through your consciousness.

Surround yourself with the white light of the Holy Spirit (or God, or however you address the Higher Power). Sit with your feet flat on the floor, your back comfortably resting against the back of the chair. Loosen any tight clothing. Place your hands upward on your thighs (this helps you open yourself up to receive grace). Take a deep breath to begin the relaxation response. Then breathe regularly, as if you were going to sleep. Cement your intellect and emotions together.

Begin at the bottoms of your feet. Feel the relaxation moving upward to your ankles, your calves, your knees, and your thighs. Say to yourself, *I want to unstress myself; I want to move all the way up the trunk of my body and every organ therein. And with each breath I take, I feel the energy and the healing and the power coming through.*

Peace and tranquility are yours for the asking. It is not a complicated formula. All the way up to the neck and down the shoulders, upper arms, lower arms, hands, and fingertips. Up through the face, the mouth, the nose and eyes.

The relaxation process may also include one or more colored lights. Generally, you would bring these lights upward from the bottoms of your feet and rinse away any stress, anxiety, fear, or other negativity. Green is the color for healing. Several of the meditations in this book show how other colored lights can be used for various purposes. At the end, always bring yourself up and all the way out by counting to three.

The possibilities and the benefits of meditation are unlimited, so relax and enjoy!

EDITOR'S NOTE: The name "Azna" is applied to Mother God at times in these meditations, "Om" to Father God.

weekly
meditations

1

the security raft

I want you to feel yourself floating on your back in warm water, unafraid. Looking up at the sky and the clouds, you feel at one with God. However, your eyes soon get a little burned and your back gets tired. But you are not too sure about turning over, because you are not sure you can swim. You are in a quandary, as we are in life: Keep floating, or take a chance and turn over?

The thing is, on your back, you can't see where you're going. Everything is out of perspective, just as in this life. It is very disenchanting, this singular view that does not give the whole truth about where you are. There is no landscape, no connection to the earth. In your mind, the intellect and emotion are fighting, as they constantly do. Is it better to float, or not?

You cannot relax. Are there rapids ahead? Trees along the bank? So you decide to turn over—you don't know what else to do. And all of a sudden you can see both sides of the shore: the trees silhouetted against the sky, the rocks, the current's soft eddies, and the deer on the river banks.

It all seems to come toward you. You start to sink, so you begin dog-paddling furiously. And you realize that no matter how exhausting this is, it is far better than floating, being nothing. As you get more tired, a revelation suddenly comes: Even if you *do* sink, it was worth it just to catch a glimpse of all the beauty around you.

Just when it seems that all hope is gone, a raft comes toward you as if pushed by a giant hand. You are so exhausted that you almost cry with relief as you grab the raft. What a wondrous feeling of security—what exhilaration. As always, it is you and your God, alone. And at your darkest, most exhausted moment, there is a raft.

This raft is what all of us are to each other. It shows the rider all the different views. We hold on to the raft as we grasp hands and love and care for each other.

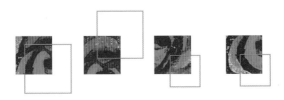

2

the duality

I want to discuss a basic truth that is too often ignored; meditate on the following during the coming week and see if it does not change your entire outlook on life. It is this: *Everything in nature is reproduced dually.* All the ancients understood the power of duality. Only Earth's patriarchal societies have created unbalancing schisms.

If there is a Father God, then there is a Mother God. If there is a divine male principle, then there is a divine female principle. It must be so. Think back to all the times when you've heard that humanity was created "in the image and likeness of God"—surely this concept of duality has occurred to you.

If you want to become more psychic or increase your control over your creative force, you must come to grips with this point: that your individual makeup is both feminine and masculine. Furthermore, if you are in a female body and you are made of the Mother principle, then this has even greater ramifications. We must recognize that each and every woman and man must pray to and give homage and respect to both the feminine and the masculine principle that is outside us. Reciprocation is a spiritual necessity.

If you do not aspire to glorify and strengthen both the feminine and masculine principles, you are only going to make yourself lopsided. Then you will never truly move ahead spiritually.

3

blessing of the mother

This is what we call our Morning Enlightenment, although it has nothing to do with morning. It's just called that. Feel yourself on cool grass. You are walking toward what we call the Hall of Enlightenment. This is a very Grecian-looking building with walls of gold.

I want you to feel your bare feet going up the steps, then see a huge blue room. A wonderful blue light emanates from an area near the ceiling. I want you to feel yourself now, just yourself. No one is there except you. You begin to advance toward a gorgeous golden beam. You are aware of a light and a presence. At first when you approach, you don't feel it. But as you get closer, you feel a golden light emanating from the beam. The top of your head begins to open, and you bask in the familiar light of the Father before you. You have always loved Him, and you feel His unbending, unyielding love for you. Now His arms extend, and you feel Him enclose you; your heart swells with your feeling for God the Father, and the love that you and He share.

Be careful to keep breathing, because during this period of ecstasy, you may forget to. As soon as you step back a few steps, you are aware of the gorgeous figure of the Mother God. Here, the warmth is much friendlier. It is much closer, and the hug is more friendly, because She is emotion. You reach up, and She embraces you in Her arms. There is such a warmth and love that emanates, coupled with beauty and motherliness.

You step back and feel a golden key of love emblazoned upon your chest; it has been pressed against you from our wonderful, glorious, blessed, omnipotent God and Goddess. They love you with an all-encompassing love, and nothing you ever do will diminish it. The joy of that love makes your soul sing, and takes away all the worries and anxieties of everyday life.

4
the lotus

Place your hands
upward on your thighs
and relax. As you go into
this meditation, you are
going to say an extra prayer
for anyone you can help with anything. You
are going to blend with the circle of other
people around you to create love and healing
right now. I would advise you to tell anyone for
whom you say a prayer what you've done
next time you see them, and see if they don't
feel a lift to validate it.

Bring a silver curtain down around you. But
do not let the curtain be open-ended at the
bottom—make an imaginary knot that goes
beneath your feet. Then open up the curtain,
making it a silvery, gossamer circle. And leave
it open at the top where, right above you, a
golden pyramid appears with the point centered downward toward you, and the mouth
pointed up. This is a filter and an infusion. As this
silvery, gossamer curtain swirls around you, I
want you to concentrate very strongly on having a seed pod right in the middle of your solar
plexus. As you do this, I want you to take a
deep breath, and filter the beam of gold

6

from the pyramid right down through the very top of your forehead, right down to that pod.

The seed pod is a beautiful, rich, velvety brown. As this beam of light shines upon it, it begins to open into a lotus flower. The beautiful petals of this flower have a fuchsia tint with a purple spot in the center, and they lift upward. The lotus was revered by the ancients in Asian cultures for its beauty and protection.

Now, right in the center of your throat, picture a green bud. It is pierced by golden light and blooms into a beautiful rose, faint pink at first but gradually becoming brighter crimson until it is a gorgeous velvet red. Feel the sacredness of these luminous flowers, and luxuriate in their aroma, which permeates your entire being. All the while, the gossamer swirls around you and beneath your feet.

a mantle of love

Return to the silvery curtain of light from the previous meditation. Feel your flowers bloom. See your curtain begin to unwind and link up to the curtains of other people, keeping a large tent of light at the base. It is pearlescent in the center and opalescent in its reflection. Begin to circulate it through the whole room, very slowly at first, then whirling so that each and every one of us, including you and me, is caught up in a tremendous vortex of colored light prisms. And this protective light pulsates back and rejuvenates us.

Now, in your forehead there is an incredibly tiny, reddish-colored bud that, as the golden light hits, becomes a velvety green leaf, then two, then three. The leaves fan out beautifully. Your main chakra is emerald green; it is now in prime health. You now feel a very large brown pod in the reproductive area. This is the life-giving chakra. The golden light that pierces it becomes a pure white rose. And the leaf that springs forth has wondrous purity and protection.

On your right side, you now become aware of Michael the Archangel, with sword in hand, ready to slay any dark forces present. And to

8

your left is your spirit guide, who has moved there in deference to Michael. All of you have a beautiful, permanent protection and mantle of love.

Your flowers are blooming, the golden light is coming down, and you sense the beauty of Michael's glowing face. So many of your guides are in attendance, praying for you. The pressure and darkness lift as you are infused with the omnipresent light of the Holy Spirit, which travels down. Your name is now written on a golden tablet; there is a contract between God, you, and your guide—a Covenant saying solemnly that you are a seeker after truth and light.

God bless you.

6

the purple flame

I want you to breathe, and let a surge of relaxation come right up through the very bottoms of your feet, cleansing out all illness. Demand to be rinsed clean of all negativity and anything you brought over with you from a past life that is causing phobias or illnesses. From this moment on, you are going to be just as addicted as I am to spirituality. It is probably the most beautiful euphoria you will ever know.

Sitting in a relaxed position, just ask for a bubble of light to surround you. And I want you to visualize yourself sitting in the middle of a purple flame, which is engulfing you almost as if you were sitting in the center of a lotus blossom. Purple is the most spiritual color. Once your mind and spirit are together, your body follows suit.

This purple flame rinses out any negativity or past-life overlays that you are carrying. You release any past feelings of hurt, vengeance, victimization, or isolation. As the light vibrates, it cleanses sickness out of your body, mind, and spirit. Say to yourself, *My spirit can never be sick. Disease is only an overlay. I now drop that from me with the power of the Holy Spirit and the Christ Consciousness.*

Now, energy courses up through the very bottoms of your feet and through your calves, knees, thighs, and the trunk of your body. Every organ is cured and healed. The light now travels to your shoulders, arms, hands, and fingertips; now it goes back up to the throat, face, mouth, sinus cavities, eyes, and the back of your head and neck. I want you to demand that the last vestiges of any illness, phobia, or fear be released right now through the power of the Holy Spirit.

From this moment on, you will get better and feel more dignity of self. You will love yourself.

the gold and purple lights of the divine

Nothing disturbs you. Nothing bothers you. Feel yourself go into a tiny room, small but not closed off. Sit on the floor of this room inside yourself, and feel the presence of the Divine. You are a spark of the Divine. This feeling begins to push upward, and the whole room is filled with light that radiates through every part of your physical being—which is nothing more than a faulty vehicle at best. But it houses your spirit, so you will keep it running as best you can for as long as possible.

Let that light rinse out all your problems with finances, children, in-laws, living situations, fear of the unknown, or the fear of being hurt. Rinse away all phobic terrors. And in this room, begin now to bring in, one at a time, those whom you wish to protect. Bring in those who need betterment in their lives, and those whom you wish to heal. Let that light bathe the sick, the ill, or just people you want to protect or remember. Bathe them in shafts of gold and purple light. All are illuminated.

Feel yourself to be omnipresent, and feel the truth that lies within your own heart—your Christ center, your Gnosticism. All the ravages of fear, antagonism, and revenge begin to drop away. Nothing will hurt you.

8

the
healing
lab

Surround yourself
with white, gold, and
purple lights throughout
your body and the atmos-
phere. Begin to breathe
in very deeply and feel
the power. When every-
thing is relaxed, feel that
you are opening up the
very top of your head.

Energy is coming through
and spreading golden light
all the way down through your head, face,
and shoulders as if it were golden chocolate
or honey dripping slowly down your body,
encompassing and healing you. And you feel
strength; you feel no fear or anxiety. You are
breathing in and out, sensing a quiet peace.
You feel the light drip down your back, thighs,
knees, and ankles; you are now suffused with
the golden, liquid feeling of quiet peace.
Nothing disturbs you. Nothing bothers you.
You are cocooned within the light.

And I want you to feel the color blue. Blue is tranquil, peaceful, and calming. Now take a bright green light, and put it right down the middle of your torso where all your chakras are—the pineal, pituitary, thyroid, pancreas, and reproductive chakras. As the green light moves down, you relax even further. You are descending on an elevator: Ten—feel yourself going deeper. Nine—nothing disturbs you. Eight—the God Consciousness is growing. Seven—the spirit is moving within you. Six—no illness is in your body. Five—your breathing is regular. Four—drop in. Three—two—one—zero. You get off the elevator, and there is a blue carpet that feels marvelous beneath your bare feet. You pad down the hallway until you get to the door. "Knock and it shall be opened to you," as Jesus said.

Push open the door, and enter a beautiful blue room. In the ceiling is a circular stained-glass skylight with the colors of gold, green, white, purple, and blue. You walk into the room and are very aware of a gurney in the center with a white sheet. You hop on the gurney and lie there staring up at the beautiful stained glass, which begins to move, to rotate. And there is sunshine behind that stained glass. Now the colored rays of light hit you like pinwheels: First the blue—royal, strong, and calming. Gold—spiritual and high-minded. Purple—

14

the highest form of all spirituality, bringing your God-center intact. White—for purity and the Holy Spirit. Finally, green circulates through your whole body, healing every infected cell.

Out of the shadows step your guides, doctors who can heal and administer to you. They lovingly approach the table and put their hands on you, holding and caring for you. They touch every affected area of your body, perhaps including places you are unaware of. In this healing lab, you are made vibrantly well by their hands.

Allow the colors to spiral and circulate through your whole body. You can put anyone else who is ill into this lab, and through your visualization they can experience the very same healing that you just did. You feel so at peace; there is nothing to fear. You are never really alone, although you may feel that way—may be born, live, and die unattended—but you are not alone. Our world is populated by spirits who love you and by a God who could never stop loving you, who holds you constantly in the warmth of His heart. Also, a Christ Consciousness emanates through you, and a Holy Spirit penetrates every cell.

Say to yourself, now, "I am healed and unafraid. I am fervently inspired. I am whole, positive, and loving. I am healed and unafraid."

9

jesus and
your spirit guide

You are walking along a sandy cliff. As the
mist starts coming up from the water below,
you suddenly feel Jesus beside you. The two of
you begin to see a pathway down the cliff to a

beautiful beach. When you reach the beach, you sit off to one side on the sand, each leaning comfortably against a palm tree.

Jesus places his hand on yours, then looks to the side and walks over into the shadows. He brings out a beautiful beam of light. This beam, you realize, is an entity. A spirit. As these two walk toward you, you recognize this spirit. It could be a loved one from the past, someone who has gone over before you, or your spirit guide. Feel the love coming. Jesus puts your guide's hand in yours. Clasping hands, you feel a surge of energy that is the love of God.

A part of you is witnessing this scene from above, this amazing spiritual communion here in the sand. Up here, you can feel the love of God the Father and of the Mother Goddess, who is called Azna. Feel the warmth of this wonderful, loving family. And down here on the sand, take a few minutes to quietly talk to your guide. At this moment, ask about anyone you know for whom you wish healing or about whom you have a question. Silently converse with your guide for a few moments.

Come back to this place anytime you wish, and feel the wind blowing on your face and the sun beating down. This can be your private chapel away from home.

the rainbow forest

Breathe deeply and relax. Feel the quiet peace. All of a sudden, see yourself standing upon the meadow floor, coming upon a beautiful glade of trees standing in the sunlight. As you approach the trees, the green, leafy boughs seem to part to let you in. As you go, feel the sunlight filtering through the trees, casting green shadows on every part of your body.

Feel the quiet peace; you can hear a few birds in the distance and smell the greenery and the earth. The aroma of flowers hits you, heady and so very strong. Smelling gardenias, roses, and pine, you walk in farther. The branches keep opening until you get to a circle of huge sentinel figures that stand almost like a cathedral. As you look up to the sky, you see the figure of the Mother Goddess, our beloved Azna, looking down on you and giving you strength. She descends through an opening in the treetops and hands you a golden sword of cour-age, love, will, and judgment.

As the sun moves, prisms of color begin to descend upon you. First, a deep and beautifully spiritual purple rain falls, lighting all the terrain. Then a golden, almost iridescent rain falls over you and you feel its touch. Now a pure, white dove comes down and hovers above you as it did over Jesus, and your voice says, "This person I am pleases Jesus."

The Holy Spirit envelops you, and the colors crescendo down, suffusing you with the love of Mother and Father God. Energy comes up through the soles of your feet, and you come all the way back up to your conscious mind. All through the coming week, the dove will remain above your head as you remember this magical forest glade. Keep Azna's sword in your hand to cut away all ties of negativity.

unconditional love

Surround yourself with the white light of the Holy Spirit. Put all your loved ones whom you want healed within this circle of light. Also, include those who have seemingly been your enemies—wish them well and bless them. Ask that anyone who has hurt, cheated, or defamed you be bathed in light.

Ask that our loving Mother and Father God show you very clearly the path of your own righteousness. Although you know of the sacrifice involved, invite the will of God to work through you so that you can experience more deeply for God. You have sustained many hardships already—poverty, prejudice, hurt, or adversity.

Feel these challenges become like golden bricks inside your soul that make you strong and cause you to stand upright. Know in your heart that without adversity, you would not have learned. Feel it so softly, the grace from Heaven, like raindrops on your face washing away all the pain, hurt, sorrow, and even the ignorance that has been perpetrated on you. You will always stand for peace, goodness, and every person's right to their knowledge.

As you stand there, a shaft of golden light hits your face. You see in the clouds above you the figures of Jesus and Mother God, and the warmth of Father God envelops you. You now have the courage to go out and unconditionally love both yourself and others. You will just *be*, now that you have a sense of whom you must be. And you will do it proudly.

12

the
pyramid
and
the
healing
lights

Think of an upside-down pyramid pointing right at the middle of your forehead chakra, which is infusing you with light, love, and conviction. You are adept at whatever you wish. The pyramid gives you the energy to do it. Bring that golden light into your hands. With this light flows a gift that turns your hands green and gives you the right to lay your hands on anyone to bring about healing and health. Forgive yourself for each of the things that you think you did, should have done, or didn't do. All you need is the God within and the God without.

Think of yourself now as a golden light in a dark wilderness that gives total and complete sanctuary and love to so many weary travelers, so many people who have taken up the lance of dislike and fallen on it. Be there for your loved ones and for anyone who needs you. You will not be drained. In your everyday life, throughout each day, try to share some of that light's essence with your co-workers, children, and everyone else with whom you come in contact. Wherever you go, let it shine. Let love, sanction, and tolerance shine out of you with complete forgiveness and grace. Send it out to those in need today.

Let that light shine into every corner of your life. All our lights infuse together and spotlight the heavens in order to please God. Before we finally leave this "boot camp" called Earth, there has to be a light in the sky. This is our way to show it.

Think of warm water coming through the very top of your head, rinsing you and cleansing your insides of all toxicity, all darkness. Rinse it all the way down your body. Stand there with this warm, wonderful, life-giving force rinsing over your entire body, warm and comforting, baptizing you. Feel every part of your body knit and heal.

Now, start to bring yourself up with the energy of the Holy Spirit. Keep that golden light with you all through the week.

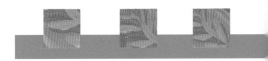

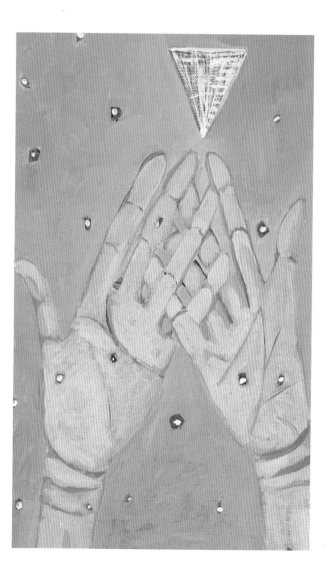

the amethyst crystal

Put yourself in a relaxed state. Close your eyes and feel that you are one unit of brilliant golden orange, which is encased in a beautiful swirling green that appears on top of the orange. Now, I want you to think of a huge amethyst crystal dropping down from the sky; its light encompasses you. From that crystal, you begin to feel the power of God because the gem is like a large, broad-based obelisk with a finger pointing directly to the sky.

God's lightning-like love electrifies this crystal. The healing vibration of God's power radiates down the gem and conducts energy into your cellular structure. It heats your body up, cleansing you of all illness, pain, and mental suffering.

Let go of all the hurt, guilt, neglect, and rejection you've experienced. Let yourself go and release it. Instead, share in the beauty and love of God, which is omnipotent within you.

Feel the energy of God's finger moving right down through the power of this gorgeous crystal that gives God's unconditional love. You are rinsed clean like a baptism.

Bring yourself up to an energetic state. May God's holy light shine upon you. May you stay in grace and walk in love.

14

baptism

In your mind, lie down on a very beautiful, white brocaded couch surrounded by soft, billowy cushions. The room recedes into velvety darkness, and you are gently spotlighted as you relax. Since you cannot see anything around you, you feel suspended in midair. All your senses are deprived of any other color, but the darkness and the white glow beneath you. This, of course, is very much like what is happening in your life. However, now you are going to receive golden cords with which you can stabilize what we might call the rocking of your essence.

Even though you might have been in trepidation, holding tightly to the cushions, you now begin to see golden ropes attaching to the couch. They swirl gently, twining up into the air. And as they do, you feel a sense of love and security. The ropes twine and rotate, thickening until they become pillars. They surround you, and inside the golden pillars the white light expands, flooding your being and purifying you. The light expands until you are submerged, baptized in an ocean of holy light, rinsed until you are pure.

Feel yourself coming back now. Put yourself on the couch, and then get up from it. As you do, you feel a force coursing through you, purifying, nurturing, loving, and energizing you.

15

the white dome

Put your hands upward on your thighs. I want you to sit up very straight. Surround yourself with the white light of the Holy Spirit. I want you to feel God's grace surrounding you, and to feel the golden light of spirituality moving through every single fiber of your being. I want your heart to open up tonight to the Christ Consciousness. I want all the old guilts, fears, and pains to dissolve away. I want the essence of you to come into full being—the unique perfection that is your God-center.

With each breath you take, begin now to exhale and let it go. Know that you are now suspended in time and surrounded with the love of God, which holds you warmly. Mother God, Father God, the Holy Spirit—all are descending. You are encased in a beautiful white dome that lights up the darkness. Your energy is now spreading out like sparks of light and is going forward to all darkness in the world.

It spreads out to all people, although most of them don't even know your name. You are sending them your love and energy and hope. Somewhere, someone senses this love while pushing their cart through the fields. She doesn't know from where, but in her heart she feels a warm spark. This may also be felt by the home-less, or those living with AIDS.

As you bind yourself together with all of these people, you are miraculously cut loose from any craziness, illness, or dysfunction. You are free from that.

You can bring yourself up now. Begin to feel all pain ebbing away. Feel it leave you. As the golden light of your soul begins to rise up, you can bring yourself all the way up to total consciousness and face tomorrow—and all the tomorrows after that.

God love you—I do.

the silver star

I want you to close your eyes, take a deep breath, and see a dark and velvety sky. As you relax, feel all your cares, worries, tensions, heartaches, and disappointments fading away. Rather than feeling cold and forbidding, the perfectly black sky feels warm and comforting around you, almost as if you were seated on a brilliant purple throne. As you sit and look at the beautiful sky, suddenly a tiny bright dot appears. This glowing, silvery-blue light begins to come toward you. As it approaches, you can almost feel its power breathed into you as energy. And more important, more than ever before, you experience intellectual acuity, manifested by piercing splinters of this gigantic, starlike light.

As this marvelous, crystal-like star comes closer, you feel the emanation of the power of God coming right toward you, then passing through you. It leaves you with the love of Mother and Father God. The God-force allows you to release all your ills and pent-up feelings, especially those from past lives. You are being cleansed of all doubt and all fear of any karmic experiences that you have not yet fulfilled. Let it sanctify you and make you whole. You came down to this world in reverence, to be a light in the darkness, and to proclaim God for the world to see.

As the star recedes, you begin to sense the dawn approaching. The tiny streaks of orange and purple now streaking across the sky signify the dawning of Mother God and the balancing of sacred energy. A beautiful love, beneficence, intercession, and unconditional love is now spreading toward you, borne on the beautiful streaks of light, which are the fingers of Mother Azna. Breathe in the colors, the scent, and the light. This is the dawn and rebirth of your soul.

God bless and keep you until I see you next.

17

grace from god

Anytime you feel divided internally, I want you to think of yourself in an egg, round on the sides and oval at one end. You are bathed in white light. Now, the white light turns green, creating rejuvenation within every cell of your body. You feel purpose, determination, fervor, and spirituality, yet you still feel that you are questioning and learning. Now, I want you to feel and sense the color blue. The only time that you should use a very intense, royal blue is to calm down any mental irritation or disruption. You experience gold, white, and green, and now the switch turns and you have purple, which gives you all grace from God, higher purpose, love of the divine, and the conviction of your inner spirituality. And right above you is the feeling and sense of the totality of Mother God with Her arms outstretched, pulling you near. You get so close and feel that warm embrace.

Pull yourself to Her breast and feel the beating of Her life-force surging through you. Her love is a creative force that constantly gives . And right behind Her, you feel the intellect and constancy of God the Father. Feel the loving embrace of both. Feel their light shining out and permeating every single cell in your body. This is the Holy Spirit—their love descended upon you. Then, because you were made flesh, the Christ Consciousness arises inside you.

You feel that you can breeze happily through the week, full of love. You are a strong, powerful, determined soldier.

18

enlightenment:
our father's gift

Feel all sense of fear leaving you. Feel the white light of the Holy Spirit, the golden light of Christ, and the purple light of God all around you. Within these lights, wish a wonderful blessing today for our Father in heaven as well as everyone around you. For Azna, our Mother God, see a beautiful rose light descending over everyone. Feel all your "plugs" being pulled out—all your fears and prejudices, all pain that spirals darkly through your soul.

Feel the healing light searching through every single cell of your body, transforming pain to joy. Azna's beautiful pink light swirls through us with the purple, gold, and white, making our souls well. They give us the fire of the Holy Spirit to go out and be examples of light, letting go of the transgressions against us. If you have recently gone through a period of anger, unforgiveness, or vengeance, let that plug now come out. Sometimes we need righteous anger, but we also need to let it slip away from us. Give it up to God; let Him forgive, and let yourself be free. Be steadfast, loyal, cognizant, and watchful—be healed.

Let this spirit move into your body today. Let healing come through you and out into the world.

19
healing

Take a few moments now to drench yourself in the energy of forgiveness. Forgive yourself and others; move into total peace and love. Let this spirit move through your body and into your hands. As they open, they get hot and glow. Ask now for the Holy Spirit to come— Azna's purity, Jesus' power. Have your hands heat up so this spirit of healing comes through you; everyone you touch and everyone who brushes against your aura will be healed by your hands. Ask for this gift today.

Feel your hands get even warmer and begin to pulsate. You've been given the gift of healing. You can put your hands upon yourself or others for healing. Don't be afraid. Ask for the gifts of prophecy and enlightenment. Ask for the channel to be pure. We're all prophets—all Essenes, all Gnostics. We're all seekers of truth. God has chosen us, so we are very blessed. And we can't get off this well-traveled path—we have been chosen, so there is no going back. The tragedy is that we're beating a new path, one that goes through ignorance and weeds and fear. But we're strong.

For as long as you're around, you must carry that banner, because it's deep-seated in your soul. And you want to make the world a better place. We want to make souls well—to turn darkness into light wherever we go. Feel that light come on, burning through you; feel your soul begin to magnify. Feel that your heart is healed and your soul grows strong.

20

the circle
of light

Surround yourself with white light, and today more than ever, lift up your heart. Feel your heart, body, and mind lifting lightly toward God. Feel the light of God descending upon you, and ask God to show you exactly where your circle is.

Revelations from God are available to you. Within your heart, feel commitment. Rinse out any fear of aging, illness, destruction, or death—even the fear of hope. Give to God completely and totally, in the same way that God's light is given to you unconditionally.

Feel the Christ Consciousness move within your heart; Mother God is protecting you, and God the Father is holding us all in the palm of His hand, omnipotently supreme. Give it up—the pain, the hurt—to the Holy Spirit, which is God's light that descends upon you.

Know that we will all make it through this, and we will all be on the Other Side together. Envision a baptism, a confirmation of our Gnostic Christian faith. We, like the early Christians, are pioneers—crusaders in a world of darkness. And we will not give up; we will stand tall and profess ourselves before God and all humanity.

Feel the light shining upon you in the name of the Mother God, the Father God, the Holy Spirit, and the Christ Consciousness. God bless you and keep you, and pray for me as I pray for you.

sail with your spirit guide

Let the white light of the Holy Spirit surround you, and envision a gold light around that. All of a sudden, you are on a large ship. You are not afraid; you see the sky and feel the ship coursing through the water, which is filled with jumping dolphins. There is something about the sky and water that brings about serenity. It's nature at its fullest. You move to a different part of the ship because you want to be alone with your thoughts and feelings, simply feeling the air against your face. You sit on a bench, looking up at the sky, and you notice a slight chill, so you pull a blanket close to you. You feel purified by the gold of the sunset, the blue of the water, the white of the clouds. The salty sea air makes your mind quiet and tranquil, taking away the hubbub of everyday life.

Suddenly, someone approaches and sits next to you. You feel so peaceful that the intrusion is almost irritating. You are internalizing the beauty of the sky and the water, pulling it all into you; then you become aware of this presence in the chair next to you. A hand reaches out and touches yours, and you immediately, reflexively, grab it. You look into the face of your spirit guide—your messenger-companion, what my spirit guide, Francine, calls a nudging spirit—who came up so unobtrusively, so calmly, from God. You feel the warmth of your spirit guide's hand, and long with inexpressible force to stay. But you are called back to the main deck of life—the reality of living—although you know full well that someday, when you cross over, you will be able to sail on this very ship, just as easily as you'll be able to fly.

Keep this image in your mind with the brilliant blue sky, fluffy white clouds, the dolphins jumping in the aquamarine waves, and the chair that is all yours, your niche.

22

reinventing
yourself

Imagine a purple flame right in the middle of your solar plexus. Ask for the grace of God to start coming down through the very top of your head, as if you are in an inverted pyramid. The bottom is closed off to negativity, and the top is open to spirituality and grace.

I want to give you a code word now—the word *blue.* During the week, any time you get agitated, say the word *blue.* This code word will relax you, calm you down, and make you feel at peace and unstressed.

Close your eyes and take yourself back to age ten. You don't need a special day, but you could choose one if you wish. Christmas would be nice. Did you make any resolutions? What happened to them? Was there anything you wish you had done? Or perhaps something you thought you had to do? Whatever it is, release it now. Let it go. This age is very pivotal; it is when your individuality begins to rise up.

At age ten, what did you look like? How did you act? What were you doing? Were you bright? Did you act stupid? Did you feel good, bad, guilt-ridden, scrupulous, frightened, abused? Did you care about things, or did you feel apathetic? It doesn't matter; release it all. The only expectation to keep is that you are going to fulfill your theme; keep your spirit guide around you; and be loyal, grateful, loving, and caring. Cleanse yourself now.

Take yourself to any age, and release the expectations that you had at that time. Take some time and relive each age—release any illness that started, any heaviness or load you began to carry. Let go of any feeling that you may have hurt someone; they wrote that contract with you. The road of your own experience has been long, but it can be joyful.

On the count of three, bring yourself all the way out, feeling absolutely marvelous.

balance, stability, and love of self

Begin to mold your essence into a round, hollow tube through which the divine light of God, the Christ Consciousness, and Mother God all shine directly down. All pain is cleared away, and you are centered in intellect and emotion.

Say to yourself quietly and with vehemence, "I love myself. I am part of God. I am God. My intellect and emotion are totally intact. I need no other human being in this life to make me contained. Anyone else is perfect; they are an addition and an added bonus. I do not need them, although they add to my already rich and full life."

Feel the thread of golden light coming through the top of your head. It threads down through every single organ, healing as it goes and taking away any blocks.

The grace from the Holy Spirit is spreading now, all the way down through your entire body. And with each breath you exhale, demand that you let go of your needs and obsessive wants. Feel these releasing. I do not mean that you should give up your dreams—those keep you going every day. But let go of the things that hang you up. Let that go completely.

Stand before God, clean and fresh. Know that our journey is with each other, and you are the hand that reaches. When we are gathered together, we can do wondrous things. Our power melds together and we can heal. Together, we are committed.

the road map

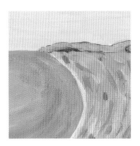

I want you to visualize a map with many roads. I want you to mentally stand up and look down on this map; along those lines, you see your grade school years, that awkward growing-up time, rejections, lost loves, some gained loves, maybe your high school or college, and perhaps a marriage or a time of independence. Stand where you are, and see how your road has unfolded. See how it forks, bends, and turns.

Now, put yourself into your life where you are now. The length behind you does not matter, but what *does* matter is what you will do with the length in front of you. Look behind you and see how far you've come. See how strong you've been in putting up with the "slings and arrows of outrageous fortune." And the infamy that you've had to put up with—the scandal, hurts, and injustices. Say to yourself now, *The only sin in all the universe is not being good to myself.* Love yourself and be good to yourself, because only then can you be good to everyone else.

Resolve to stop feeling "unworthy" or not good enough. No one should feel that way, because we are all genetically part of God. If there is any evil, that is it: you defaming you. Yet how easy it is to fall into this trap. Negativity is the slime of the earth; it grows as easily as mildew after rain. It is imperative to breathe fresh, clean air because you are a child, an instrument, the moving hand of God.

See your map, your road. You charted it out, so smile through it. Love and commit yourself along the way. Feel the breath of air from God filling your lungs, renewing your tired body. Forgive yourself now, and feel forgiveness for as long as you wish. Being in the body is a terrible strain, because your soul bangs against it. But you will thrive.

Feel the hope and love that arise from standing together with hands outstretched. Feel the energy right through the bottoms of your feet, rising through your entire being, and shining out through your head.

symbolic
roadblocks

Begin to feel yourself relax as you go down
an escalator. This is your lifeline, where you can
now open up your channel. This is where you
can get in touch with your guides and get your
messages. Count backward: Ten—let yourself
go. Nine—all systems work better for you than
ever before. Eight—let go of all negativity.
Seven—bring in God's grace through the top of
your head. Six—with each breath you exhale,
feel the negativity leave. Five—go deeper.
Four—breathe more regularly. Three—two—
one—zero.

I want you to imagine yourself in a field.
Feel the wind on your face and the grass flop-
ping against your legs. And you feel the power
of the spirit move with each gust of wind, tan-
gible and strong. Visualize that you are surrounded by a glowing white light. Feel it about
eight to ten inches from your body, glowing
brilliantly and protecting you. In front of this
field, I want you to see every negative thing
that's ever been in your life beginning to rise
up like symbolic roadblocks. Name each of
these ugly brown blocks: anxiety, neglect, fear,
illness, rejection, pain, the inability to express

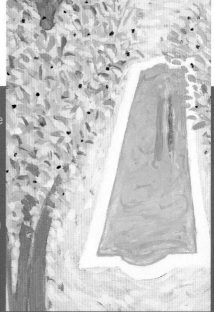

yourself, and so on. And let these blocks build, because we have all got them looming in front of us. They hold us down to Earth and block us from God.

Now, reach out in front of you, take the light that surrounds you, and hold it in your hand. You can pull it out from your arm just like a snowball. Throw it at the blocks with all your might. Watch them crack, crumble, and disintegrate. Furiously and more furiously, you throw these, until all blocks dissolve and become dust.

And there you stand—a wonderful, beautiful, God-centered being, totally in control and totally willing to do whatever God wishes you to do. Free of all judgment and guilt, you are standing and breathing free.

ring of power

I want you to now reaffirm the power of Almighty God, the true Christ who walks with us, the love of the Mother Goddess that surrounds us, and the omnipotent Father God, who is our Maker and Creator. And put a ring, a circle, in the middle of the room in which a beautiful, white, sparkling shimmer of light begins to form. Around it forms a purple sheath of light as a curtain. Now it is almost as if the shimmering circle turns into water and takes on shades of blue and green. I want you to mentally see a golden light shining directly down from Father God.

Close your eyes, take a deep breath, and put in the names of your loved ones to heal them through the Christ Consciousness. Mentally put in your own name if you so choose. Put the names into this shimmering, beautiful, emerald green healing water. Wherever these people are, a ladle will be dipped out by Azna's hand and administered to them, whether they are with us or separated physically. Reaffirm tonight to God Almighty: "I am well and strong. I am spiritual and blessed. I possess the Christ Consciousness and the love and strength of Almighty God. I am on a mission in life to redeem myself and others spiritually. I ask this in God's name. Amen."

Feel the empowerment of God coursing through every cell in your body. Every part of your being that has been darkened or left unattended is now surging with the light and brightness of God.

I leave you with blessings and protection. Know that if you ever call on me, I am but a tiny thought away. God bless you.

the bridge

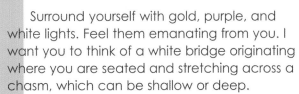

Surround yourself with gold, purple, and white lights. Feel them emanating from you. I want you to think of a white bridge originating where you are seated and stretching across a chasm, which can be shallow or deep.

Astrally, get up from your chair and begin to cross that white, glistening bridge over the chasm. As you do, take all the guilt, hurt, and physical pain you carry, put them in a plastic bag, and throw it over the side. This action merely cuts your ties without causing harm.

Do not feel alone—you walk this bridge with strength. You hold on to both sides and are sure-footed. No wind rocks the bridge; nothing can hurt you.

As you go, think to yourself, *What's the worst that can happen?* You can die. Is that the worst? That's easy. But no matter what happens, you can walk that bridge. Now you turn around—and you are amazed to see others walking behind you on the glistening white bridge, throwing over their garbage bags. Some have huge, yard-sized Hefty bags, and others have very small bags. All are filled with, "I didn't get that job that seemed so great. I lost my lover. I wasn't what I wanted to be." Let it all fall over—push it away from you and walk proudly across.

Now you get across to the field, and feel thinner, lighter, and brighter—more in tune with the infinite. This is because God is now channeling through you. You can open up your heart and connect with Him, Her, Jesus, and the Holy Spirit. Let all that grace rush in from all the powers that be—the Archetypes, your spirit guide, and those that have gone before you. How protected you are.

Now you go back across the bridge. As you cross, you look over the side, see all that "stuff," and know that it will never come up again to haunt or hurt you. As you cross, you feel lighter and brighter, filled with conviction about who you are and what you believe in.

28

a blend of light

Bind yourself with colors of light. Now, start blending them. Begin by threading a white light through your forehead and into your throat, solar plexus, and lower intestinal tract. Next, thread a purple light through the same path. Surround yourself with this bubble of light.

Take a gold light and thread it through the same path—your forehead, throat, solar plexus, and lower intestinal tract. Now take a green light through. The light is now around you in its rainbow of colors.

You should do this every day—it takes only a few minutes. Ask that your emotion and intellect be cemented together and that the white light of the Holy Spirit surround you.

I promise you that if you ask Father and Mother God as well as your spirit guide to protect you and your aura, then your aura can go out into a pain-filled desert and conquer it.

29

healing
embrace

I want to take you on a journey. Surround yourself with a purple light—the royal color of spirituality. Both you and I are asking for rows upon rows of people to all come around you in a circle, to bless and care for you—your spirit guides; the Archetypes; everyone whom you've ever loved and who has loved you, whether in your past lives or this one; your dear pets who have passed on; children that you've lost; fathers or husbands who you think are not there.

A mist appears and hangs heavily around you. You're a little afraid to walk because you can't see far in front of you—much like this life. However, you feel warm hands on you and the love of a mother or grandmother who comes

56

back. You feel them press you to move forward. All these people surround you now, and you are standing in a beautiful meadow. The love emanating from this group is such a strong force that you are actually borne up by it, and you float freely above the circle, enjoying unconditional love and nurturance.

In the meadow, you can see white-maned horses frolicking in the distance among trees bearing luscious fruit and profusely flowering bushes. You feel the desire to be closer to all those who surround you, so you float down and feel their warm, loving hands touching you, pulling you close in embraces. You feel the physical warmth of love. A green light seems to emanate from them; it heals you, sweeping up slowly and thoroughly from the bottom of your feet all through every area of your body to your head. Feel your father's arms around you. Feel your mother's kiss soft on your cheek. Feel your spouse hold you in his arms. Feel your brother come up beside you and lay his hand on your shoulder. Speak to them. Breathe in the fresh meadow air, scented with wildflowers. Now return to your body and look straight ahead. Notice how revitalized you feel.

Each time you do this, I promise you, you will be healed completely.

three circles of
infinity

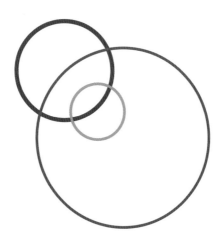

See yourself walking now through a beautiful silver tube. As you walk, the most marvelous thing happens—it's almost as if the tube vibrates sparkles of light. Elated, you begin to skip a little bit, amazed at these silver sparkles that seem to purify you as each enters your soul. At the tunnel's end is a light in the shape of a beautiful cross. The light emanates gold.

In front of you are three golden circles that represent your total, infinite, God-centered self. One is God the Father, another is the Mother, and the third is your own divine consciousness. You join the circle with the divinities and feel yourself part of the golden loop that is intertwined and linked. Now, as you pass through this golden tube, feel your guides become present on either side of you.

Right in front of you stands a gigantic amethyst crystal. Go over and touch it— the purple light resonates in your soul. Touch and feel it. Ask it to send any messages it may have for you. Ask for forgiveness—but not from God; ask that you be able to forgive yourself. Ask for the ego to be slain like the dragon that it is. Invite your truest "I am" to come forward. It will. And slay the dragons of illness and hurt, despair and grief. Feel your relaxation. Breathe in the purple glow, as well as an emerald glow from another gem nearby.

You can visit this beautiful vision many times and carry it with you. Bring yourself back through this silver tube of light, carrying the amethyst and emerald glows with you.

31

ebb and flow

Feel warmth, the white light of the Holy Spirit, and the Christ Consciousness moving around you. Feel the presence of your own emotion and intellect. I want you to feel the love of Mother and Father God. All heralds of truth attend you, along with your spirit guide and the Archetypes.

Feel like the ocean—feel the ebbing of all pain, heartache, disappointment, and fear. In their place, white foam comes on a wave and rinses away everything but a shining silver light. Let this rinse over you like a baptism. The healing that comes leaves you free of all fear—fresh, clean, and alive.

From this moment on, you will live by your own truths, your own God-center, and whatever makes you happy during this spiritual journey of survival. Let the ocean's movement rinse away all regrets and leave you fresh, healed, and flooded with the grace of God. Feel the strength of your soul now magnifying and stretching.

The tide ebbs and flows—the pain and grief recede—not just for now, but for the future. Feel your strength rise up. Once the outer crust is removed, all bigotry and prejudice will be washed away.

Standing before God, you are cleansed. You are healed. In the state of becoming, you are perfect, spiritual, knowing, and God-centered. Take a deep breath, and let all your pain and disappointments go. You are bonded to a sisterhood, a brotherhood, which will survive and be strong. This group is not intimidated by life's fears.

Begin to feel energy rising through your feet, cleansing, healing, and burning out pain and sorrow all up through the body. You are strengthened, and your destiny and wishes are fulfilled. You feel marvelous from head to toe—better than you've ever felt before.

a s h o w e r o f s t a r s

I want you to see, behind your eyes, a beautiful glowing star in the night sky. This star is blue, as they so often seem when we look at them. There are shoots of red, white, and silver around its corners.

Now, you are not just looking at it; you actually *become* part of it. You are the star; it is inside you emanating the magnitude of your soul. Your greatness and beauty are now radiating. Also, the star's points are pushing out any and all negativity. To an outside observer, it might appear that you are streaking downward, but you are just gently descending in the dark sky.

At first, in the fall, you feel afraid and somehow lost. You feel isolated. But hush! In this dark sky, you seem to feel the refraction of light, and you look over and there is another star. Lo and behold: As you look behind you, there are lots of stars falling with you.

Your star does not intercept the light of others. We are falling together, shooting out our love of God, right action, nonjudgment, even a feeling of passivity. We are streaking across the dark world with the light.

Listening closely, you hear little yelps of happiness, because together, we make a big, huge light. The other stars join our cluster, and we feel the bond of starlight that even joins the Star of Bethlehem, showing the light, the way, and the truth.

Notice your feeling of contentment and deep peace, your sense of will, and your judgment center. Feel the strength of your backbone, insulated from the "slings and arrows of outrageous fortune." Feel the quiet peace and the benediction from God, Mother Azna, Jesus, and the Holy Spirit that surrounds us.

Go out from today with peace in your heart, and try to get someone else to pick up the thread. God love you.

the golden key

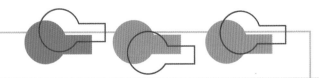

Affirm the following: "I shall never be swayed from my true spirituality. It is beautiful, blessed, loving, and filled with all goodness. To relinquish this blessing would be to turn to ignorance."

Carry this golden key with you, pressed into your chest. It has been bestowed upon you by our blessed Mother Azna. Feel that you can pay witness to what you believe, and please pay witness to the God of Love. Speak of Him often to those who may not want to hear. Not that you necessarily want to convert them, but stop the onslaught of pain and terror that is brought on "in the name of God."

Stand in witness to spiritual beauty and truth—this is the golden key. Nothing you will ever know is any closer to the truth or any more precious than this.

Carry this golden key of knowledge with you. You carry a golden sword, and now a golden key as well. You move down into mundane life, knowing that you can reach this peak of spirituality at any time you wish. You can come back to this blessed height, speak to God, and be with Him any time you choose. There are no certain times of the day when He is tired or less receptive to you. He is at your beck and call, residing not only *in* you but *outside* you.

Be free of what you call sin and guilt, totally neutralized in your own beauty. Amen.

the candle

Today and throughout the week, really make this a special time for Christ Consciousness and for appreciating Father God's protection. Think of a candle giving light, infusion, brilliance, and the warmth and grace of Jesus; these fill every single part of your heart and soul. Feel yourself walking the same dusty road that he walked, giving out his message and dispersing love and goodness. Feel his caring and love for his fellow human beings.

The candlelight begins to have a halo around it, which burns away all worries about yourself and your family, health, money, car, and household—all those worries and things that you carry with you. Let them all be rinsed out, because all things pass away. It is all a dream, and you can make it a fun one. You can laugh at the inequities of life.

Feel yourself being reborn, and resolve to love yourself more and more. Take the edge off your impatience, and realize that the true reason for your life is to experience for God.

Feel a rainbow of color now spreading through you—the green of healing, the gold of Mother Azna, the purple of spirituality, and the white light beaming down. Feel deserving of the love that you have for yourself. Stop all petty jealousies and worries. Let go of the hurts that have been put on you, and realize that it is all part of living. It is all part of  the flesh. Forgive yourself for any transgressions that you believe you have acted out.

Ask to remain on track in this path, now that you have caught the hand of God. Let Him take your old overlays of behavior. Give them to God, who is always there for us, static and omnipotent. If you do this, you will never be alone again because your inner peace will always be with you. Warmth surges through you, taking away all pain and fear. Keep this light around you, and every single day this week, try to do one unselfish thing for yourself. Because when you truly love yourself, you will be able to love all others. And they will feel it. God love you.

let the spirit move through you

Surround yourself with white light; put gold light around that, and purple around that. Feel yourself breathe in these ribbons of color, and let negativity out. These white, gold, and purple ribbons instantly hook you up to the divine, your God-center, and to the God we serve and love, Who holds us gently in the palm of His hand.

Feel love travel down those ribbons of color and go right into your heart, threading through your mind and releasing all guilt. Say, "I forgive myself," even if you feel that you have nothing to forgive. Do this because you have been so inundated through all the centuries with guilt. The spirit of God moves through you and is constantly there with you, never critical or judgmental. Pray that you will become more and more like this as you move through your life. Give nourishment to your own life and the lives of your family and friends.

These strands of color now thread through your whole body—down through the throat, torso, spinal column, digestive area, buttocks, and legs. This color, this feeling of love and God-centeredness, will endure. Your intellect and emotion are cemented together so you are impervious to being attacked by anything, even yourself. Allow yourself total self-control. Do not ever give it up to anyone else for salvation, love, caring, or your existence. Promise yourself that *you* will take care of, and love, yourself. Promise that you will no longer be tortured or victimized. No one can hurt you anymore. You can do this without becoming uncaring, unfeeling, or unloving—of course you can. Say, *I forgive myself, love myself, and am in control of myself.*

Feel the energy coming up through your entire body, from toes to head. You come up feeling absolutely marvelous.

festival of the lights

Become aware that your soul is now stretching, moving, expanding, and majestically
magnifying the Lord. It reaches far out into the
sky, and you can feel the air rushing by your
face. The farther up you go into the ebony sky,
the more aware you become of tiny stars all
around. As you get closer, you see that they
are not stars at all, but beautiful white-robed
entities. Archetypes and past loved ones are
coming toward you with lighted candles. And
you are rushing to meet these Hosts of Heaven.

You see these glorious entities and your
guide standing there in gold, white, and purple
robes. Their lit candles show their warm, wel-
coming, smiling faces. As you draw closer, you
feel the protection of all the Gnostics and true

Christians who have gone before. They pass to you all synergism of love, all loyalty, and everything tried and true.

Above this, the Queen of Heaven appears, golden and shining, Her beautiful long hair is a glowing mantle on Her head. Her purple cloaks blow in the breeze, and you feel yourself surrounded by the peace and tranquility of God. You offer what is in your heart—your thanksgiving and even your sorrows. Bring them up, and with the wave of just one candle flame, it all passes. Today's hurts are tomorrow's forgivenesses. They all sink into a deep well. And you feel, in your soul and heart and mind, that your candle has been lit by the Trinity.

Carry that light out of here, and pass it to everyone you meet. Give off the light of love and the richness of your true belief in a loving God and Goddess, not the feared God. The loving, constant God smiles on all of us tonight.

sending out love

Let yourself relax. Let go of your whole
body. As your senses draw inward, I want you
to feel your soul elevating, stretching, and
moving higher. Feel energy coming up through
the soles of your feet and rejuvenating you.
See yourself standing beneath a dark sky, surrounded by the souls of all your loved ones and
protectors on the Other Side. You feel their love
and caring, see their shining faces break into
smiles at the sight of you, and receive their
embraces. They form a band of protection so
that no one can hurt you. No one can send

negativity to you. Anyone who wishes ill upon you cannot penetrate this barrier. You feel borne up by this caring and love; you feel stronger than you ever have before.

With this force and strength inside you, you now release it to others. You send your love and caring to all the people who need hope and help tonight. As I tell my people, send out your love, and in some dark corner of the world, someone will catch that love from the spark of your candle, although they may not know it. As we light our candles together, we create a light so large that it can purify this whole world, wherever we may go.

Feel this force of love and healing pulse through your body; you are receiving love and sending it out. Feel this pulse travel through you; see the healings occur. Now bring yourself all the way up. And this week, go out and do something selfless each day. Let your actions as well as your spirit heal others.

God love you—I do.

the well-traveled road

Ask for the power of Mother God, Father God, the Holy Spirit, and your Christ Consciouness to envelop you. And I want you to feel yourself walking in a field that is bright with flowers. The wind is blowing. Suddenly, as you are walking, you are aware that there are others walking with you. Some are running behind you, some to either side, some are skipping in front of you, and some are holding hands with each other and with you. You all go along, exhilarated, enjoying the warm and beautiful day, eager to see where you will finally end up.

As the day progresses, the sun gets high, then begins to drop. You notice that there are not many chuckles, laughs, or footfalls around you. You look around. Is it your imagination, or are there fewer people with you? Well, you could have been mistaken. The sun sinks deeper, and the beauty seems to disappear, yet you are determined to walk on. It gets darker, and now you are utterly alone. It is scary, but you know that God and your guide are there, although not visible. You walk alone with no one to really pour your heart out to, or to walk with you.

Then in the half-light, almost like a hologram, others begin to walk with you. Shadowy at first, but shoulder to shoulder, you are walking together. Maybe these are not your first choices for companions—maybe they are strangers to each other and to you. But there is something about the eyes, the handshakes, the hugs, that speaks of sisterhood, of brotherhood. As a group, you have traveled this road for thousands of years and will do it again.

You feel calm, knowing that there is a spiritual homecoming. All pain washes away, all hurtful things that have been thoughtlessly spoken. Forgive those people and let it go. Walk on and feel the golden light of Christ and the God Consciousness filtering all the way down to your toes. Keep this light all through the week, and forevermore.

commitment with god

I want you to surround yourself with lights. Start with an emerald green; above that, put a beautiful purple light for Azna. Now add gold for the Christ Consciousness, and white for the purity and protection of your own soul. Feel truth and righteousness in the depths of your soul.

Open your heart to the love of God. Open your soul, and let all vengefulness that is in the world today rinse away. Be affirmed. Be committed. Be constant. The soul needs a constant vigil. Let the golden, purple, white, and green lights flood through your soul.

Feel the mantle of She who is truly our blessed Mother flowing through you. Feel the strong arms of our Father and the living, breathing Jesus who walks with us. Ask to be healed of all programming. Feel the hurts soar and uplift. By the love of God, you now do good works, volunteer to go out and help the poor, and open your doors and rooms to all those in need.

Feel the peace, love, sanctity, and grace. Your soul now lifts to God almost like a quiet, flowing rinse. Reach deep into your mind and

dredge up all past pain to be released. Let it all go, all of what you thought was sin. And what rises up is all righteousness of what is good and clean. When you go before God, you are shining and bright, freed from all fetters of ignorance. You come to God with not only love and emotion, but intelligence as well.

Feel the channel opening so that you infuse directly from Mother and Father God. Nothing stands between you. Make a commitment that you will march through this earth, cleansing it and bringing people to the knowledge that they are good, kind, and pure. Tell them that God loves them and that He does not inflict hate, harm, or vengeance. God does not take babies because He is mad. We are only here for a time, during which nothing matters but our commitment to God.

wings of the mother

Close your eyes, and lift up your mind and heart to God. You are going to see both Mother and Father God because they are together. Azna is the blessed Mother Goddess who comes down to help with everything. Feel Her love and Her wings of warmth enfold you. The dove of the Holy Spirit, which is the symbol of my church, appears above, and your commitment and belief in the Christ Consciousness is within you.

Ask Azna, God Almighty, the Holy Spirit, and the Christ Consciousness to rid you of all negativity—to drop it, to chip it away. Ask that Azna's wings of hope, love, and divinity surround you and keep you protected. Meditate on Jesus' meaning when he said, "Mother, behold thy son. Son, behold thy Mother."

The symbol of truth and consciousness is Azna, our dearest Goddess—our Mother with Her mantle of protection. She intercepts in our lives; all we need to do is ask Her for help. Consider your deepest request now. Ask the Mother for that which is in your heart. Do this now.

This week, stay in contact with Azna. Glorify Her and pay her homage. Once you are beneath Her wings, She will help you in all areas of your life.

the grecian temple

I want you to take yourself to a beautiful, Grecian-looking temple. Move past the massive columns and open its doors. Now feel, sense, and visualize Jesus coming up on your right side. You see his reddish-brown hair, large brown eyes, and his beautiful hands raised to touch you. He is tall and slender in a garment of white and purple, and a beautiful golden light surrounds him. With him is Azna, the Mother. They hold an image of infinity in a beautiful light beam. To their left is our own Father God, who is called Om, and a beam of light. Here is the true Trinity. When Christ touches you, you feel the embodiment of health. Put yourself in this circle, along with anyone else you wish.

From the top of this Grecian building, you see sunlight shining through stained glass. Seeming to move and rotate in the sky, the sun hits amber, green, orange, blue, and gold light. It keeps rotating so that each one of these colors fills your heart kaleidoscopically, sanctifying your being. Above all, you are given the truth of your own intellect, whatever that may be.

Your yearning for God lifts you up divinely so that you touch a part of God. Sanctified, you can now ask for your life to be easier, because you are on the right track. Ask that from this day forward, negativity should not hit you, even if you must deal with it. It will not be a part of you, but will be dealt with as if through a Plexiglas barrier.

Ask this in the name of Mother God, Father God, Christ, the Holy Spirit, and your own Christ Consciousness. Bring yourself up now all the way, feeling blessed, loved, protected, and so full of grace.

God bless you and keep you.

the golden steps

Placing your hands upward on your thighs, I want you to surround yourself with lovely white, gold, and purple lights. Ahead, you see beautiful golden steps. Mentally push yourself forward to the steps. From a distance, they seem impossibly high, but now that you are closer, you see that they are not too high for you to climb. Take each step one at a time, lifting your legs high with each step.

Perhaps your feet were muddy and you smudged the first step a little. However, the mud soon wears away, and now you look down and see that your feet are clean. They are sparkling, and you feel that your back has become straighter and your head is held higher.

You keep going up, one step at a time. It gets hard in the middle of a long path, and your muscles ache. You forget to look up. You keep looking at the steps, and then you suddenly see the figure of Jesus waiting, arms outstretched, brilliant light engulfing you and him. And on each side of him are the Mother and the Father. You suddenly seem to have wings on your feet, and you can easily ascend each step one at a time. You fly higher into the heart of Jesus.

Jesus is with the Father in His constancy and the Mother who cares for us. Surrounded by the Trinity, the light of the Holy Spirit emanates, rinsing your heart of guilt, sin, and hurt. You are made strong.

Ask for your heart to be made open to decisions. Ask for guidance on how to lead your life to its rightful conclusion. Ask how to stop the fear of death, and how to look forward to going to the Other Side. Feel God's love rush in, clearing any negative blocks. Feel true spirituality and grace flowing through every vein and capillary. You are forgiven and rejuvenated. You are full to bursting with courage, power, and the strength to go on. You can do what must be done.

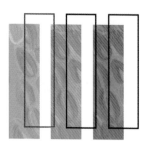

43

the power lines

This meditation was received from my spirit guide, Francine, during a trance session. It is included because of its powerful impact, for the benefit of those who wish to get in touch with their Christ Consciousness.

I want to do a meditation for you. I want to show you how to line up the power lines. There are an awful lot of guides and Archetypes surrounding you right now. I have no idea why we are so filled; this must be a very spiritual group. The room is just packed. I have watched them come in all evening and surround this whole room.

Mother Azna is with you, and She is surrounded by every messiah: Jesus, Mohammed, the Buddha, the Divine Messengers, and every divine being. Now I want you to bilocate yourself and go join these messiahs, because that is where you truly belong. You are messengers sent here directly from God to pass the Word. Directly above you, you feel and sense the omnipotent presence of Father God. He takes on the presence of being very tall, with shining, diamond-sharp blue eyes and beautiful gray hair with no beard. You form a cross with the Mother, the Father, and all the messiahs.

Come back to this cross formation anytime you wish to escape from your often harrowing, disgruntled society. You can experience union with the Creator and the feeling of light and love, peace and release. You are blessed with honesty, truth, and the knowledge of why you are here. You will minister to the truth, as your soul dictates. Ask God to bless all those not with you at present. Ask Him to shine His beauty, love, and healing down on those who persecute you.

Feel the blessings of this. Feel the blessings that I also extend to you to help you deal with those who hurt you. I promise you in Azna's name that they will soon be released from you and pay homage to you. All love and healing comes filtering through.

the
temple
of
quiet

On the Other Side, the Temple of Quiet is
shaped like an octagon and is quite ornate.
The floor looks like marble. As you advance to
the center of the room, each block that you
step on begins to emanate a light. It is almost
as if each of your footsteps creates a shaft of
light coming up. It is quite lovely—with pinks
and mauves, purples and greens.

When you get to the center of the room, ask for resolution of any problem you may have. Now, a beam of light goes right into your Third Eye from a crystal set into each wall of the octagonal room. When this occurs, the problem begins to be enacted in front of you like a hologram. You observe from the perspective of your higher self.

You see many options for dealing with this aggravation or concern in your life. You can now program the ending exactly as you desire. If you are very quiet, you will see the option that has been eluding you. For example, if you do not get the job you think you want, what do you choose to move on to? If you cannot get along with a certain person, ask God to show you several options; ask that they be enacted in front of you as if on a movie screen. Choose the one that feels best to your higher consciousness.

It is often very beneficial to see the worst that can happen played out in front of you. This can really help you dispel fear and feel in control. You can then reconstruct it so that it works out as you want it to. This fulfills the great conglomerate plan.

the egg
of
the mother

Close your eyes and take a deep breath. I want you to put yourself into a golden egg, a golden ova. A purple band streams all the way around this egg, like an Easter egg. It pulsates while you sit inside, cross-legged and with your thumb and index finger forming a complete circle. Do that now with your fingers, as priests have done in ceremonies of communion. This gesture is powerful in any situation because it makes one circle. Use it when you are in any stressful situation. Now begin to breathe in green so that your organs receive healing, energy, spontaneity, and refertilization.

Directly over this egg is Mother Azna with Her mantle, as always—beautiful in Her power, gorgeous in Her glory, golden in Her suffusion of light. This egg is the symbol of Her power. Inside it, you are completely protected.

This egg is surrounded by the Archetypes. When you imagine them, know that you are creating very real imagery all around you. See these very tall, blonde, sentinel figures who report directly to God; they are standing around you and giving you electrical currents.

You are inside the egg, but it is almost as if you can look out of it and see Mother Azna spread out Her mantle and Her arms, forming wings that shelter you. Golden and beautiful, She can create any miracle She wishes. Your atmosphere is suffused with Her mantle of light. She gives love and forgiveness to all, and understands any unforgiveness you may have. She gives you complete and total sanction to be.

music and colors

You feel brilliant sunlight shining directly on you. You are enveloped by Our Father in Heaven, and Mother Azna is with you, wielding Her golden sword and taking away all pain. Moving your mind laterally, you open its channels wide and clear. You go back to a morphic resonance of when we all lived as Gnostics with pure knowledge and belief, and no dogmatic authorities.

You are sent a crescendo of color and sound and beauty; it permeates every single molecule and cell in your being. The colors and music seem to have a life of their own, flowing through you. You feel yourself affirming, "The music of my soul resounds to the touch of the divine. In sound and color, my spirituality has risen to new heights, and I am at peace."

You are imbued now with courage, fortitude, and perseverance; all those nitpicky human and worldly cares are rinsed away. You feel your spirit rise and touch God. And forever after this moment, your soul will never be separated from God, because it has touched the divine, which will live with you for eternity.

moving forward

Feel yourself standing quietly on a seashore. Feel the breeze blow against your face and the warm sand beneath your feet. Think about all the things you worried about before you came here—how little they matter now. You are just standing before God; the two of you are simply together. "Nothing tainted," as Cyrano de Bergerac wrote with his unsullied white plume.

In God's presence, your deepest self arises and shows you the path in front of you. You know what action to take now in order to move forward in your life.

If you are in a rut, plant seeds. If you are on a high and grassy hill, mow the grass. And if you are atop a mountain that is brown and barren, scream out your love for God. The atmosphere and the universe will hear you.

Feel all the cares and all your tiredness and nit-picking go away. Know that we are always together in our hearts and minds. You are the reason that I am. Neither of us is ever alone. We may not see or feel those loving, caring entities that surround us at all times, but in our spirits we know that they are forever walking with us, guiding our steps.

God love you—I do.

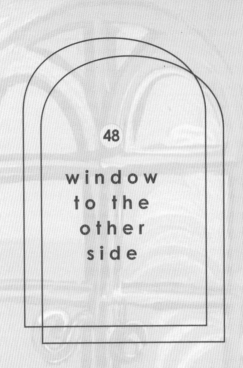

48

window
to the
other
side

Close your eyes and breathe deeply. I want you to feel a golden light around you. Around that is a glistening silver egg. It is almost iridescent opal, prismed with light. And you are cocooned inside, sitting in the lotus position. As you sit there, this prism of light begins to change colors, turning gold, green, blue, and several shades of purple. The purple now seems to bathe you in the light of spirituality. Feel it move through every cell of your body.

From your lotus position, you now lift up your face. The purple and gold lights bathe through, and you stand and stretch. Your arms extend freely out to their fullest length. Suddenly the visions of Azna and Om, our Mother and Father, appear on either side of you, blessing and loving you. In front of you, a hole forms in the iridescent egg and becomes a window.

Through the window, you see the green grass and the hills of home. You see the Other Side's sweeping meadows and beautiful rose-colored light. At that moment, all the loved ones who have passed before come toward the window, reaching out to you. You cannot yet reach them, but you can put your hand through the window and touch the ones from whom you have been separated. You see their faces and feel their love, which they are sending to you. See how much they care. They are waiting for you, because you will always be together. By this reality, they give you grace.

That picture dissolves, and in its place the beautiful opalescent egg surrounds and protects you. I want you to walk around with that egg for this coming week. You will not ignore that which you don't want to see, but for a while, you will keep yourself sequestered to heal. Then you can break down the sides. Keep it close so that for a week, your soul is allowed to expand in this cocoon. You are still loving and giving, but no one may hurt you or spoil your ideals or the reality that is you. Feel a healing quiet, and never feel alone.

rebirth

The figure of Jesus approaches, wrapping you in his arms. And the Mother God is here with Her beautiful sword and shield. Of course, Father God is constantly and eternally present. You feel all the love of the Trinity pouring through you, lifting you and holding you warmly, close and protected. For a few moments, you feel almost lost in the beauty of all this as you are suffused with sparkling laser beams that hit your body, and, passing through, cleanse it of any illness or deterioration.

The miracle of your rebirth has started. You are now miraculously impervious to any dark force. Your depression lifts, and the iron mantle of distress dissolves into light. You will now function perfectly at work as your thinking gets clearer and your aptitude increases. This is a tiny touch of what it is like to be on the Other Side.

Take up the sword today of righteousness and truth. This will get you through the coming week, and all your life thereafter. Within your heart, spread light to everyone you have ever touched—even those who have done you wrong. God knows how hard it is, but let's spread the word of what this world is really and truly about.

Ask this in your Christ Consciousness and in the name of the Mother and Father God. And now, feel the energy coming up all through your body, from feet to head. Affirm: "I will truly be a light in a lonely desert, enlightening many."

50

the
tree
of
knowledge

You are in a field. You're warm, although it is a little overcast and the wind is blowing. There is nothing in this whole field except a beautiful tree to your right. The wind begins to nip a bit, so you move toward the tree's spreading branches and massive, solid trunk.

Approaching, you can feel the energy of this tree. You move right under it and feel compelled to hug and hold it in the absence of any other living soul. Suddenly this tree, which has always stood for knowledge, becomes almost electrified. You feel as if the branches could enfold you. The branches, the trunk, and the spiraling leaves go upward toward God. And you know that you can meld with this Tree of Knowledge and search on your own—it will be the most magnificent search that you'll ever have. You are seeking your own spirituality. Let all your "stuff" fall away—any feeling that you ought to be poor or humble or deprived, for example.

You are not asking for any more than to simply subsist in your soul. Feel all your questions being answered, because you are now quiet enough to listen—just quiet enough to open up. Your meditation will now be profound enough to hear God's voice. My spirit guide, Francine, talks about how tragic it is that people do not believe that God has a voice, so they never tune in to listen.

Feel the grace pour down over you. And bring yourself out all the way, feeling absolutely marvelous, better than you have ever felt. You have a feeling of completeness.

51

past-life
meditation

This meditation was taken from the book
My Life with Sylvia Browne,
by my psychic son, Chris Dufresne.

Relax your body. Concentrate on breathing. Relax your feet, ankles, calves, thighs—all
the way up your body. When you are totally
relaxed, take yourself back to, say, age 20,
or any age you can comfortably remember.
Keep going back in your life by ten-year inter-
vals, focusing on specific incidents, no matter
how important or trivial. Take yourself all the
way back to your conception. Then ask to go
back through a tunnel of time into a *valid* past.
The tunnel is white, and then you see yourself
bathed in purple light. Now, see yourself looking at a map. One place will jump out at
you from that map. No matter how far-fetched
it sounds, *take your first impression*. Leave the
word *imagination* out of this equation—just go

with every first impression you get as you begin to ask yourself questions: "Do I feel male or female? Am I young or old? Where do I live? Am I rich or poor? What is my name? Is there anyone with me in this past life whom I know in my present life? What is my life's plan? Did I learn from it? What maladies am I suffering from? How did I die in this past life?"

Ask yourself as many questions as you can think of, and just go with the experience and the answers you get. Make a mental note ahead of time to remember this "journey," and write it down in a journal afterwards. Also, while you're in that past life, ask that any negative cell memories, which you may have carried over, be dissolved in the white light of the Holy Spirit. Conversely, ask that any positive cell memories from that life be brought forward. And *always* add the codicil that any pain that should be tended to by a physician will *not* be alleviated, so that you can and will be responsible for getting it taken care of.

52

rites of autumn

I want you to spend time relaxing yourself completely and surrounding yourself with green, white, gold, and purple. Get in touch with God's knowledge. Now, as you exhale, go back through time to a life long ago, when we were Gnostics in the Qumran group. The women are all wearing freshly washed mantles of linen, and the men are draped in off-white or dark colors. We are gathered together on a grassy knoll in the middle of a desert, facing a huge statue of Mother Azna, roughly hewn of stone by our artisans. There is danger in having such a statue because some outsiders consider this idolatry. Yet we bravely live by our beliefs, because as She anoints us, we become shining lights in this desert and in our lives today.

In our rough muslins and sandals, bearing baskets of food, our hearts are full of petitions. We want to be steadfast, and to be able to

share every part of ourselves. As we approach, we feel a freshness. A light rain begins to fall as the sky clouds over. Mother Azna is not crying, but She is sprinkling our heads with holy water. We feel soothed and blessed with each drop of rain that moistens our faces. We are being anointed; our pain and our cares all drop away as if we were all one being, and our courage arises within our breasts. It is almost as if the statue in all its beauty becomes supple and alive. Azna descends from Her pedestal and reaches out Her beautiful arms; She dips Her fingers into a golden chalice of oil and anoints each person here. Say, "Mother, help me to remain constant in my fervor, and let my actions reveal my innermost beliefs." Feel the quiet breeze as an anointing; feel Her forgiveness.

To the ancient Qumrans and to us, this anointing means that you are marked by Her, which is probably the most beautiful gift you can ever have. As Azna stands and Her beautiful eyes shine out at every one of us who ask to see Her, miracles are created constantly. No one can forgive everything, so always ask for Her blessing upon those in pain and those whom we cannot forgive. Let Her see our shortcomings. Release pain by giving physical comfort or giving monetarily. Let us help our loved ones to sustain grief, and let us help each other through the journey of life. You are anointed; feel the strength and abundance in your heart.

About the Author

Millions of people have witnessed
Sylvia Browne's incredible psychic powers
on TV shows such as **Montel, Larry King Live,
Entertainment Tonight,** and **Unsolved Mysteries;**
she has also been profiled in **Cosmopolitan,
People** magazine, and other national media.
Her on-target psychic readings have helped
police solve crimes, and she astounds audi-
ences wherever she appears.

● ● ●

Also by
Sylvia Browne

Books

Adventures of a Psychic (with Antoinette May)
Astrology Through a Psychic's Eyes
Conversations with the Other Side
God, Creation, and Tools for Life
Life on the Other Side
The Nature of Good and Evil
The Other Side and Back
(with Lindsay Harrison)
Soul's Perfection
and . . .
My Life with Sylvia Browne (by Sylvia's son,
Chris Dufresne)

Audios

Angels and Spirit Guides
Healing the Body, Mind, and Soul
Making Contact with the Other Side
*The Other Side of Life: A Discussion on Death,
Dying, and the Graduation of the Soul*
Sylvia Browne's Tools for Life

Hay House
Lifestyles Titles

● ● ●

Flip Books

101 Ways to Happiness, by Louise L. Hay

101 Ways to Health and Healing, by Louise L. Hay

101 Ways to Romance,
by Barbara De Angelis, Ph.D.

101 Ways to Transform Your Life, by
Dr. Wayne W. Dyer

Books

A Garden of Thoughts, by Louise L. Hay

Aromatherapy A–Z, by Connie Higley,
Alan Higley, and Pat Leatham

Aromatherapy 101, by Karen Downes

Colors & Numbers, by Louise L. Hay

Constant Craving A–Z, by Doreen Virtue, Ph.D.

Dream Journal, by Leon Nacson

Healing with Herbs and Home Remedies A–Z,
by Hanna Kroeger

Healing with the Angels Oracle Cards (booklet
and card pack), by Doreen Virtue, Ph.D.

Heal Your Body A–Z, by Louise L. Hay

Home Design with Feng Shui A–Z,
    by Terah Kathryn Collins

Homeopathy A–Z,
    by Dana Ullman, M.P.H.

Interpreting Dreams A–Z,
    by Leon Nacson

Natural Gardening A–Z,
    by Donald W. Trotter, Ph.D.

Natural Healing for Dogs and Cats A–Z,
    by Cheryl Schwartz, D.V.M.

Natural Pregnancy A–Z,
    by Carolle Jean-Murat, M.D.

Pleasant Dreams, by Amy E. Dean

Weddings A–Z, by Deborah McCoy

What Color Is Your Personality?,
    by Carol Ritberger, Ph.D.

What Is Spirit?, by Lexie Brockway Potamkin

You Can Heal Your Life, by Louise L. Hay . . . and
Power Thought Cards and *Wisdom Cards,* by
    Louise L. Hay (affirmation cards)

All of the above titles may be
ordered by calling Hay House at
the numbers on the next page.

• • •

We hope you enjoyed
this Hay House Lifestyles book.
If you would like to receive a free
catalog featuring additional
Hay House books and products, or if you
would like information about the
Hay Foundation, please contact:

Hay House, Inc.
P.O. Box 5100
Carlsbad, CA 92018-5100

(760) 431-7695 or **(800) 654-5126**
(760) 431-6948 (fax) or **(800) 650-5115 (fax)**

Please visit the Hay House Website at:
hayhouse.com
and
Sylvia Browne's Website at:
sylvia.org

You may also write or call her office:
Sylvia Browne Corp.
35 Dillon Ave.
Campell, CA 95008
(408) 379-7070

• • •